CONTENTS

PARANORMAL PUFFIN:
VOLUME 1
By Jake Thomas

The following is the transcript of the first nine episodes of my podcast Paranormal Puffin. The information presented is a mixture of my own personal experiences along with what I could find through google searches and the various topics presented. I invite you to read through these pages and learn with me about various paranormal, supernatural, folklore and cryptids. In this book you can learn with me a basic understanding of The Shadow People, orbs, the wampus cat, selkies, Scotland's Fyvie Castle, Austria's Moosham Castle, The Philadelphia Experiment, how whistling can summon the paranormal, and whether or not children can see spirits. So, take a moment and learn with me or if reading isn't your thing, then go listen to Paranormal Puffin wherever you enjoy your podcast!

THE SHADOW PEOPLE

Hello there and welcome to the Paranormal Puffin a Potent Puffin sideshow and I'm your host Jake Thomas. Now for this inaugural episode I'm going to be discussing the shadow people if you're not familiar with the shadow people they are pretty much just as they sound, they are humanoid figures that appear as shadows usually out at the peripheral of someone's vision. Now there's from my research there's not a whole lot known about the shadow people it's unclear exactly what or who they are some people believe that they could be aliens, others believe that they could be angels or demons, or some believe they're from another dimension or could be time travelers or just travelers from other dimensions it's really unclear, but one thing that is generally common is they usually do instill a lot of fear and a lot of those who encounter them. I've read some where they don't really cause fear they don't seem to be malevolent they don't be mischievous or appear to be evil necessarily, but a lot more often they do cause some sort of unsettlement or fear in those who encounter them and so

I just find them kind of intriguing kind of because I have had experiences myself with what I believe to be the shadow people. Had one that I'm for sure it was a shadow person and then two other encounters where I don't know if it was the shadow people or not. May just been other similar entities I'm not a hundred percent sure so I'll just start off with my three experiences or possible experiences with the shadow people. So, the first and this one kind of leaves me to think that it is possible that the shadow people could be extraterrestrial in nature but, there's a few things about this story that made me think maybe it wasn't shadow people it just happened to be a humanoid figure in shadow form. So, this one kind of starts off so this is back in 2013 um no 2012 yeah 2012. When I was in the coast guard I was stationed aboard the Alex Haley we were on our way up to the Arctic and before we proceeded into the Arctic Ocean we stopped in Nome, Alaska and this occurred the night before we pulled into Nome so we were already near Nome like you could see Nome on the horizon we were just doing like a bar pat outside of the harbor because we were there but we weren't ready to moor up because we wanted some more up during the day and so we're just kind of doing like a holding pattern basically before we go in and I was on watch up on the fly bridge doing lookout and say it was probably about three or four in the morning because it was like the one hour of darkness that we got and so I'm kind of just looking up at the sky because it's a nice night not much going on and I see what at first just looks like a regular shooting star I just you know I'm like oh cool shooting star I watch it I'm like oh you know what would be cool? Is to look at this thing through the night vision goggles so I pull up our night vision I stick it up to my eye and I'm like oh man this is cool like because you just see this star and it just gets really bright. Well then it becomes stationary and I'm like well that's kind of weird it's usually when you see a shooting star you know you just see it for a few seconds it falls, and it disappears. Well, I still get through the night vision monocle, and it just stops I'm like wow but I could still see the light from it and then it just starts pulsating like and it's just flashing like that's kind of weird and so I take the night vision down and you can't see it with the naked eye. So I go back with the night vision see if I can still see it and there it is this light still just flashing it's pulsating and then it flashes really bright and like almost wipes out the night vision and then once you can see it like the light dissipates you can see it still just there like a concentrated ball and it just starts shooting again it's going really fast and you cannot see this with the naked eye, you have to have the night vision to be able to see it and then again it stops and it's pulsating again and then this time it flashes and then when it dissipates and you can see through the night vison again it's just gone and I'm like that's kind of weird and then when it did I had this really intense sense of uneasement like something was wrong like I thought something was going to come and get me like I don't know what but I just felt like there's some kind of negative energy there and the only thing I could think to do is I didn't even think about it I just instinctively did this I turned around and I was like be gone from me devil in the name of Christ be gone and then that's when I noticed on the deck there was this humanoid shadow like there was a shadow and it wasn't like it was like wasn't my shadow like it was humanoid in shape as in there was a circle at top and then a long slender part that appeared to be a body but it was like really slender and rectangular and it had branches off where what where an arms would be and but again they were kind of like just really rectangular and same thing at the legs it was really kind of weird and I was like that is creepy and then, I

look over and there's this pair of binoculars mounted there on the deck. There's like a mount and then they're mounted up on top and they've been seized the entire time I was on board like I've never been able to move these things like they're seized stationary you didn't use them because you couldn't move them and I didn't know anyone else that could move these either at the time and then all of a sudden that pair of binoculars just swings around and I'm like this is really creepy and then I start looking at that shadow and I'm like I've never seen the shadow before but then as I started looking at it I started calming down and like whatever it was about this shadow it was actually making me calm so I don't know

I don't know what it was I don't know if the shadow was appeared and got rid of whatever was causing the negative or if it's what was causing the negative and then wanted me to know that it wasn't as negative as I was perceiving because it was unknown to me but I've never seen it before. I've never seen it before that but after that it would occasionally appear and it usually would appear at times when I needed to be calmed down so I don't know it was it's just kind of weird but the fact that it was a shadow but it was a shadow on the ground like it was flat so I don't know if it could have been a shadow people or not. But just because it with those lights in the sky makes me think that you know maybe it was a shadow person and they are of extraterrestrial origin or it could be possible that maybe there's different types of shadow people and just because we don't know enough about them yet we haven't been able to fully classify the different sects of them like maybe there are extraterrestrial ones maybe there are some that are more of you know angels demons or other dimensions they could maybe all those theories are truth to extent and it's that we've just lumped together several different entities into the same category just because we don't know enough yet and so that's about it for that encounter.

The second encounter is my most definitive to a shadow person is what I definitely believe this was a shadow person and so this one occurred in 2014 when I was stationed aboard the Kukui we were dry docked in San Francisco actually in Alameda but so the bay area I don't think the area is really much important I think it could have happened anywhere but so there's one night when I'd come back to the ship after you know going and exploring town for the day and I come back and I was on the phone with my wife and so I like to have some privacy when I do that and so I went into this one compartment where we store all of our deck tools and equipment for working the buoys it's dry dock so no one really is going there because that's just not being used and so the way it is you have your the buoy deck and then it's this one room with equipment and then there's a second room behind it with more equipment and so I'd go into that second room and you know you just be there no one would ever bother you. So I got done talking my wife and I was like all right I'm going to go to bed now. I went and as I've exited the second room, I'm in the middle room now about to go onto the buoy deck and as I'm getting ready to cross through the threshold of the door, I see in the corner of my eye something just darts past me. I'm like whoa so I turn to look and when I do sitting up on this shelf against the wall I can very clearly see a person looks like a person and they're hunched up sitting on top of the shelf but they are completely black like no face just black and it was definitely three dimensional could not mistake it for anything other than a person but it was just like completely black and it's just like a dark void shaped like a person. I could feel like it was just looking at me like I don't know for sure because it has no face, but it based on the way the body was turned it was like the head was looking at me and it was just really creepy. Like I was kind of freaked out. I didn't know what it was thinking I don't know what it was wanting to do but it was there with me, and it felt like we were locked eyes with each other and it's a little different because a lot of times uh from the encounters I've read with shadow people most people say when they turn and look it's gone. Like they say most people only see it out of their peripherals it seems very rare um, but it does happen occasionally where people do see it full on and it was weird it's just weird. But after a few seconds looking at it like I never said anything to it. It never made any noise, but it definitely felt like it wanted me to know that it was there whatever it was. Then I just kind of walked backwards out and once I was onto the buoy deck I kind of just slowly put my back to it and hastily made my way across it never it didn't try to follow me I don't think but it was just kind of weird. It was very different from the one on the Alex Haley because this was definitely a three-dimensional and I knew it could move because I mean he was in like a crouching position and I saw it in my peripheral it was dashing and then it was up in that crouching position when I saw it full on. You could definitely just feel the energy in the room at the time you could tell it wanted me to know it was there was really weird and it was definitely creepy it creeped me out I it stayed on my mind for a couple days after and yeah it definitely made me feel fear, but I don't think it was uh intending to cause fear necessarily I think it's just I just didn't know what it was. I mean and it was a military ship like it that's something that's not there it shouldn't be there so it's just more fear from just I didn't know what it was I didn't know how it got there I didn't know why it was there not necessarily like it's an evil thing it's just more fear of the unknown rather than fear of the evil, but that was just something about that that was kind of weird but to me that's one is the most definitive yes that was a shadow person it wasn't an alien that happens to be a shadow or appear as a shadow it wasn't a ghost it wasn't a it was a shadow person.

My third experience is kind of a weird one and so with this one I was in "A" school in Yorktown, Virginia and I was asleep, and I was having this very intense very vivid dream. I've always have had very vivid and very intense dreams but this one was a little different. So in this one I'd encountered a dark shadowy figure that was fairly humanoid in shape and we got engaged in battle like I was fighting this thing both verbally and physically I was fighting this thing in the dream and in the midst of it like it was causing me intense fear in the dream like it was this thing was evil like no doubt about it and I don't know what it was and it was very intense like I felt like I was sweating but when I woke up I was dry I was not sweating but I felt like it in my dream. I remember just waking up and I jumped up out of the bed and I just started yelling at this thing telling it to get out then to be gone I was like get away from me. I'm like yelling at the top of my lungs meanwhile my three roommates are still dead asleep not waking up from me yelling and I'm like well that's weird. I'm like maybe they didn't wake up and they just aren't saying anything they're just you know trying to downplay it and so the next morning I was like hey guys I'm sorry about yelling I just had a bad dream I don't know what came over me and they're like what are you talking about. I'm like when I started yelling in the middle of the night and all three of them were like we didn't hear anything like you were never yelling and I'm like in my mind I was yelling as loud as I could. So, I'm like I don't know if was just a dream. I think it was some kind of possibly a shadow person based on how it presented itself in my dream or it could have been something else and that's just how it manifested itself I don't know but it was weird it was creepy and very intensely scary.

I was talking about that with a friend of mine later on and they're like well it's possible you did in fact yell as hard as you could but that you did so psychically and didn't realize it, I'm like okay that I guess that's plausible, but whatever it did I think it worked because I don't remember falling asleep again that night ever just being awake and just vigilant. I eventually did fall asleep, but I didn't realize I fell asleep because it's I was awake and the next thing, I knew it was like I think it was like 12 or 1 o'clock in the afternoon and I was waking up. So somehow, I fell back asleep, but I don't know how long it took but it felt like forever and like it was weird because like I felt like I was sweating that was very cold, but my body was dry like I wasn't sweating and then yeah it was just a very weird experience. Like I said like I have vivid and intense dreams but nothing like this. This was different and so that kind of you know to me leads to you know I guess it could be possible that their angels or demons and this was more of a demonic one and that's how it manifested itself it could be that they are just you know either aliens or beings from another dimension and maybe some maybe angels or demons sometimes manifest themselves as shadow people because that's just how they are they think that might be a form that benefits their cause at the time because they're being able to take advantage of something we don't know about and may not perceive as being what they truly are. But I don't know that's just kind of my take on it. I'm sure I mean and I'm by no means an expert on shadow people but maybe someone who knows more could you know maybe enlighten me on their thoughts about some of these encounters I would very much appreciate it but those are just three encounters or possible encounters that I've had with potential shadow people definitely the one on the Kukui was in my mind for sure a shadow person and who knows the first one maybe um maybe it was just an alien I don't know but then again it is possible that shadow people are aliens and from what research I have done it does appear that a lot of people who have had shadow people encounters have also encountered extraterrestrials in some way. So that is an interesting connection definitely helps lend to the belief that they could be of an extraterrestrial nature or origin. But just the way when I saw that one head on just how he was just so he looked like just a void it makes me think it is possible they could be from another dimension or time travelers or just traveling for another dimension, and that void is just what's left from moving between. But I don't know it's very interesting and yeah so those are my experiences. I know there's different things about the shadow people some people say that they have red eyes and none of the ones I believe I encountered none of them had that. But it could just be you know like people there's different kind there's different you know physical traits. So, I don't see why shadow people can't have different traits from individual to individual.

I know there's one legend of a very particular shadow man called the hat man I believe, and he is always like he's not good if you encounter him, it's not a good thing. He tries to cause harm from what I can tell but other than the one from the dream none of them felt like they were trying to cause harm. The one on the Alex Haley actually I think he was trying to call me from my brain, or my subconscious maybe knew that what I was looking at was extraterrestrials but I didn't think so I didn't realize at the time but my subconscious knew it which caused a fear reaction in my brain possibly that's my theory on what happened and that shadow was I don't know if it was the extraterrestrial or it was something sent by the extraterrestrials to be like hey we know you don't know what we are. We know you we noticed us, and we know it's common for your people to have fear when they do. So, I'm just here to calm you. It could be a possibility I don't know but that's my theory on that particular one.

Now are those three instances of mine are they all interconnected somehow? I don't know it's possible, but I don't think so. I think they are just three separate occurrences that just happened to happen to me. I don't know it could be that I'm just you know receptive to these types of experiences I don't know. I mean I've talked with it with a few a few people I know that are more versed in some of this stuff than I am and they both kind of seem to think that not only from these but other experiences that I've told them about not necessarily regards to shadow people but other just other experiences they think that I might be like receiver or conduit for some supernatural or paranormal activity. I don't know if it's just me or somehow like I'm just more open to seeing it so therefore I do see it more. I don't know not that I just see paranormal all this time, but I do seem to have a good share of experiences more so than most people I know but it's just something interesting and I'm looking forward to this new sideshow of mine the Paranormal Puffin. So I can try and share some of my experiences and do some more research and share on that and it won't just be a paranormal supernatural stuff also maybe the occasional conspiracy theory um just things along that anything that could be paranormal supernatural um just really abnormal in general may get discussed on here and I look forward to this I hope y'all have been entertained. I hope you all enjoyed listening to it may be learned something you know it's kind of cool and I thank you all for listening and if you enjoy it, you know check out my regular podcast the Potent Puffin and I'll be sharing the same social media for Paranormal Puffin and be shared on the same social media so if you follow me on there. Keep following if you're not check it out cool stuff and I'll catch you guys next time on Paranormal Puffins should be a monthly occurrence.

CAN CHILDREN SEE SPIRITS?

Hello there and welcome to the Paranormal Puffin a Potent Puffin sideshow on this episode I'll be discussing one interesting question can children see spirits and are they better at it than adults? Now one thing I've noticed especially after becoming a parent is that often times children look off and will look like they're be looking at nothing, I'll see nothing that they're looking at but it looks like they're intently focused on something and my wife gets really freaked out about this because she's always been under the impression that children are better at being able to see spirits and ghosts and things of that nature than adults and that children can see things that we can't and so I've kind of paid attention to this with my own son and I've kind of noticed that. I know there this one area in our house especially when he was an infant and early toddler stages there was one area in the house where he would always just kind of look up and you see his eyes like they're following something look like he's looking at something but there wasn't anything there and my wife always was freaked out about that she always thought that you know he was seeing some kind of spirit or ghost or something and when he was an infant and he slept in his own room my wife liked having him in the room with us rather than having him in his own room with some kind of monitoring system because she was always freaked out that she would look into the monitoring system and see something with him or see him look like he's interacting with something that we couldn't see and so that's kind of intrigued me into thinking that maybe you know kids can see more than adults.

I kind of interested in why that is, and I think back to my own childhood and not necessarily seeing ghosts but I know one thing when I was a kid especially at night it even happened during the daytime and light but happened more often at night in a dark setting I could always see like these little floating dots in the room. A lot of times and it's just weird because they didn't feel like just pieces of light, they felt like they were something. I always thought you know there's something sentient about them and you know I spoke to my parents about it once and they kind of dismissed it as imagination and then the next time I went to see an optometrist they asked the optometrist about and he explained something I don't remember what his explanation was but it's basically you know just my eyes in the development or something I'm not real sure that's been probably 20 something yeah over 20 years ago that this occurred and eventually after that I started seeing them less but they've come back and I've seen them more often. I've been seeing more a lot recently too usually at night these just like floating dots but one thing I do remember is there is one time I woke up and I saw those floating dots but they actually came together in like a human sort of shape and floated above me and in the head most of these dots were black when usually I'm seeing lots of different colors uh lots of blues and greens and purples but this night they were all the dots were black except for a few that made two eye kind of shapes and what would have been the head because it was like a human and it just kind of like floated above me and it was really creepy feeling and I just stayed awake all night just watching this thing until eventually it left and it was really creepy and so I think back on that I'm like you know maybe there is something to it maybe you know younger children are more susceptible to it and so I've done a little bit of research and some of it kind of coincided with what I already thought and one theory about it is that you know children haven't been taught that that stuff isn't real. I mean I'm not saying it's not real but you know children haven't been taught and influenced by their culture by a lot of the adult culture that that stuff isn't real they haven't been told no that's not real so they their minds are open to it they haven't shut that off in their brains yet. So because they think because they see the stuff and they don't know what it is and so they categorize it as you know that's what they're seeing and whether it is or isn't I don't know but the thing is since they haven't you know programmed their mind to think that it's illogical to be a ghost or a spirit or whatever they're open to categorizing that categorizing it as that. I don't know that could be the correct categorization because I also think you know a lot of western culture kind of is like that. We say no this stuff doesn't exist it's not logical it's not what we're seeing therefore it's not what we're experiencing and eventually we just shut ourselves off to it we quit being open to it, so it doesn't present itself to us. But you think a lot of times other cultures outside of our own often have you know people who are in touch with this ghost and spirits or fairies and you know elves whatever other entities there could be and you'd think well is it reason these other cultures you know experience these things keep close with it in their mythologies and their you know and in their culture in general is it because they haven't shut themselves off to thinking that's illogical and therefore it is logical and so since they haven't conditioned their minds to think that it's illogical these things still present themselves to those people. Since children are pretty much an open slate in their mind, they're still open to the idea that these things exist. So, I think that is one possibility. Some could be you know this is just a very good imagination of the child but like I think that kind of ties in you know where does imagination start and where does it end and in my research I kind of find some interesting things. There does tend to be a spike around Halloween for reports of children seeing these apparitions and experiencing other worldly experiences and so it could be that their imaginations being hyped up by a lot of the media what they're seeing on tv reading in books because they're putting their themselves in that mindset for that particular holiday which really celebrates uh you know ghosts and ghouls and things and so they're putting their minds and you know and creating that imagination to that but it could also be I think you know they because they're putting their minds into that mode by being engulfed in extra media that maybe there's because they're young enough they're still subconsciously tapping into their minds and allowing themselves to be open to it so it could be part imagination but it could also be part you know allowing themselves to be open.

So, another thing I saw is that you know used to they would think that children had a difficult time differentiating reality from fantasies but a lot of recent study shows that children as young as three are actually very good at telling the difference I mean there can still be mistakes in telling a difference but a lot of times they're actually a lot better than a lot of adults at differentiating reality from fantasy and they're able to switch between the two very easily. So, I think it's reasonable to think if they really believe that they're seeing something otherworldly sometimes spirit angel ghost whatever it may be that if they if children are this good at being able to switch between reality and fantasy and their belief in their seeing this and I think it's logical in my mind to think that they are experiencing that.

So, another interesting thing I found is children their eyes are actually able to see differently than adults and so this may be something that is allowing them to you know see these things. One thing that I found is that you know adults they see UV lights between 400 nanometers and 700 nanometers and light becomes invisible to the human eye between 315 and 400 nanometers and so we see above that but children are capable I don't know where the age cutoff for this is but younger children can see as low as 380 nanometers and so they can see part into that range that's invisible to most adults. I know that a lot of times paranormal investigators use UV technology to try and catch and show proof of spirits and ghosts and entities because they appear in that lower range of UV light and so it could be that they do exist, but because of their light patterns they're below what's capable for most humans but they're still in that range of what children are able to see because they can see into a lower range of the UV light and so I think it's reasonable then that you know some spirits you know may hang out you know just below that 400 nanometer mark that most adults don't see but most children can see and so that's why they're able to see it. So that could go into kind of what the optometrist was talking with me and my mom about when I was younger is that's why I was seeing that could be related to why I was seeing the dots is because my eyes hadn't gotten to the point where they don't see below that 400 range yet they're still in that younger stage of being able to see more on the UV scale and so that's why I'm saying that but that doesn't explain why I felt like these things were sentient in some way and so I just think you know I was could have been seeing other things. I mean like I said they could have easily been orbs. I may discuss orbs on another later episode because they're that's a whole episode's worth going into what orbs are but that explain a lot of why a lot of times what I saw were blue because blue orbs often times relate to calming and so it's like calming spirits or some kind of calming energy and like I said a lot of times it was at night when I was seeing them and I was afraid of the dark for a long time and so it makes sense that these blue orbs might come to me at that time because they're there to help me calm so I could get a restful night's sleep. So that could be why I've been seeing them a lot again lately is I've tried to open myself more to experience these things. If you listen to last episode from last month then you know you know I've experienced um some things with potentially shadow people or extraterrestrials.

Someone explained things there and so since those experience I've tried to allow my mind to be more open and that's kind of when I started seeing these dots or orbs again and a lot of times they are in that blue shade and so it could be that they're trying to help me calm down. I have a battle with anxiety a lot and so that would make sense why these calming energies are coming to me they're trying to help me battle through that anxiety and calm me down. I've also noticed that has been happening since I've had my child so you know could be that I'm trying to allow myself to be more childlike in some way so that I can interact with my child better and so maybe there's some kind of subconscious tap there has allowed me to be more open to these things

Another kind of theory about what they're saying or who they're saying is that children are new to the world and it's possible that you know they themselves just came from the spirit world and so they're still seeing memories of the spirit world or they're still seeing remnants of it but as they develop and learn about this new world that they're currently in begin to see it less. I think that that makes a lot of sense to me, if you've ever moved from one place to another you still have memories of the place you came from and so to leave one world into a new world it would make sense that especially while you're still young and impressionable that you are still seeing memories of that old world and that's what they're seeing is they may not actually be seeing anything presently they may be seeing memories or you know things that they remembered from the spirit world or wherever they were before they came into this world.

So that is interesting to me. I did note that a lot of times the thing said one theory on who or what children are seeing is more often than not it's some relative that has passed usually a recent passing as well and they're there usually to help guide the child or protect the child and that's what they're seeing and I noticed that with my son after my wife's grandmother passed is he kind of after that he kind of had a little spike in his imaginary friends and it could be that his imaginary friends were just his way of his great-grandmother was appearing to him she was you know just checking in on him and doing so through his imaginary friends and that to me is calming it's a good thing I think i mean I'd rather know that it's something good like his great-grandmother looking after him that he's interacting with rather than some unknown entity I mean that's good and like I said it makes sense because there was a spike of it right after she passed so that would make sense to me that that's who he was interacting with through the perception of this imaginary friend. So that's something cool I mean and it's a way to keep those people alive in our minds because as long as we remember people, they're never truly gone but in a sense that you actually still know they're actually they're outside of just our memories when you're interacting with them in that way that's really cool, I think so you know I just found that really interesting

So that's about all I have on children seeing ghosts as to what they're seeing or why they're seeing it if anyone out there has their own theories I'd love to hear them or if you have your own experience of from when you were a kid or of your kids you know I'd like to hear them. You can find me on twitter interact with me there put in comments you know you can email me at potentpuffin@gmail.com you know I'd love to hear these things or if you have any you know just any knowledge you know to help me learn more about this I'd greatly appreciate it and you know yeah so I don't think it's these are initially things to be worried about I think they're things to kind of embrace because you know I think it's good that we stay open to these types of experiences. I think it helps broaden our understanding of the world and what's going on around us and so I think you know when interacting with children who are say they're experiencing things i think it's important not to just dismiss it and I think it's good that we try and you know not actually encourage it but interact with them in a way that lets them stay open and think for themselves on what are they experiencing and know that what they're experiencing is valid and not just dismiss it because I don't know it may not only cause them to shut down uh being open to these things but it may also cause you know other developmental issues um as well I don't know but some of the research I've read kind of suggests that that could be a possibility but in the end I think you know just interact with them talk to them find out what these things are you know ask them if they're telling them anything um see what they're saying like I know for a while uh my son had his happy monster as he called it and I would talk to him and I'd have like hey what does the happy monster say and he would tell me stuff and it was never really anything bad a lot of times it was just you know he had this happy monster and for a little bit he had um in another room there was a grumpy monster I think is what he called it but his happy monster kept that away and the grumpy monster didn't stay around long cause the happy monster got rid of it and so I found that interesting I mean some of that could be I don't know it could be imagination could be you know he's actually being a part of something I don't know but I thought that's interesting and you know I don't just shut it down that you know I let him you know experience and I interact with him to make sure that it's nothing bad or dangerous for him and eventually you know I haven't heard much from the happy monster lately I'm kind of its past so I don't know but it's something interesting that he's experienced and it's something that it's a good memory that I'll hold on to as he gets older and I don't know maybe he'll when he's older he may tell me more about it or it may flee from his memory as he gets older I don't know but it's still something to hold on to as a memory of when he was a kid.

But yeah like I said if you have any thoughts or you know experiences along children experiencing or seeing things of another world you know I'd like to hear it like I said you can email me at potentpuffin@gmail.com or follow me on twitter interact with me there or leave comments on my YouTube videos whatever I'd love to hear your input and I will catch you all on the next episode of Paranormal Puffin and also check out my weekly Potent Puffin as well if you're want to just go inside my weekly life and I'll catch y'all next time.

ORBS OF PARANORMAL DUST

Hello there and welcome to the Paranormal Puffin a Potent Puffin sideshow and I'm your host Jake Thomas and here in the studio with me tonight is Kita the elkhound and on this month of Paranormal Puffin I'll be discussing paranormal orbs. Now my decision to talk about orbs this month was kind of debated in my mind it was my initial idea to talk about orbs this month however on a side project that I am also working on doing some research for I thought about going a different direction but just doing a little further research both towards orbs and into the side project I decided that for right now um going with the orbs would be a better topic for now and I'm going to save that research for my side project for my side project and it will probably manifest itself on the podcast sometime in the future when that content fits in a little bit better in my mind and so this month like I said I'll be discussing orbs now the most common thing with orbs is for them to show up in photographs there's been a lot of increase in orbs appearing in photographs since you know right around the 1990s there started being an increase. I think a lot of that's due to digital cameras becoming more popular and accessible around that time and so more people were taking photos in general and so more people were you know experiencing this phenomenon with the orbs and if you're not sure what I'm talking about basically a lot of times someone will take a picture and then they'll go back to look at the picture and notice that there are little spherical floating objects in the picture that weren't there when they initially took the picture. Now there's a lot of different explanations behind this phenomenon from being spirits or other paranormal entities to just being malfunctions or tricks of the camera or to just it being you know just dust or rain or something microscopic that you couldn't see what was within the scope with the lens so I'm just going to look at some of these different things and try and figure out what these orbs are and are they paranormal or are they not. Personally, I think you have to look at each photo individually and look at other context clues to really know. So first I'm just going to go over some of the you know camera explanations involving the camera itself so basically you know how a camera works is it uses light to create a reflection of the image and it creates an inverted image based on that reflection and that's what gives you your picture and so anything you know that light could reflect off of will end up in the picture even if you don't see it so like little specks of dust or eyelashes that were sitting along the lens they could you know cause some kind of interference in the final picture and that's one of the easiest ways to write off an orb is you know there's some dust or there's a bug or there's a reflection off of you know some waters you know if it was raining that will definitely cause orbs to show up in your picture because light loves to reflect through water and you know with the rain a lot of people will see the rain drops and think oh that has to be an orb because it looks like it's traveling because you see the light going you see like the spherical base of it and then there's like a trip like a tail to it almost but that's would be expected with rain because rain is falling from the sky you know and so the most dense part of the raindrop is towards the bottom because the gravity's pulling it down but light like electricity likes to take the path of least resistance which means it's going to the light is going to exit and reflect off of the top of the raindrop where it's less dense so that's kind of what creates that tail on the orb and gives it that appearance of traveling and so that is how water kind of plays into it especially rain and you know orbs they come in all different types of colors that's why some people you know get into you know think oh it's a reflection or something you know it might be you know white or not clear you know so but when you start seeing other colors and that can you think oh it's not a flash because it's not the color of you know what you think of a flash so but that can be explained through you know different fabrics that are in the area of the picture you know because those the colors of those fabrics depending on what they are could cause reflection and reflect off to create to give that color to the orb but when you start looking at the paranormal aspect of it those colors can be of importance because and kind of tell you what the meaning behind the orb is and give you it can be a little extra clues to what's going on spiritually in that area and so going into that that is another explanation of orbs is that they could be spirits of some kind. A lot of times when talking about the spirits and those they have to have so much energy to be able to manifest themselves and so some believe that it could be a spirit with a lower energy level and that's all that they're able to manifest themselves as these little orbs in pictures but they're not able to fully manifest themselves to us because they don't have enough energy and so going back to the colors like I said the colors can give us an idea of what's going on with the area. You know if you're taking these pictures as part of like an investigation or you know they come as a surprise but you had suspicions that you know there could be you know something paranormal or spiritual in the area you know the color of these orbs could give you some clue as to what might be what these spirits are trying to communicate with you and so I'm just going to go over the colors real fast and if you've studied you know the chakra this might sound familiar some of it would be different from that as well just because of different theories on the colors but a lot of it kind of aligns with that. So, you see your red and orange orbs they're one of those that have different potential meanings it could be that it's you know trying to communicate with you that you know or something that's safe or secure about the area or that the spirit that's there to provide safety and security for you. You know it could have been you know someone who you knew or maybe don't know but they're there to protect you they're a protector a caretaker of some sort which kind of going into the other theory on red and orange can be a little scary because it could also potentially be that it's a negative energy that's angry so you really got to be careful because those are two very opposite ends of the spectrum you know it could be something there to provide protection but it could be something that's angry and you know showing itself it's red because we associate red with anger and so it's wanting you to know that it's not happy with you there so you got to be really careful with red and orange in my opinion because it could go really either way. Green orbs you know it could be something there that's you know wanting to be loving and compassionate or it could be something associated with nature so it could have been you know maybe like the spirit of like an animal or you know the trees you know could be something from nature that's gone on and it's still lingering around in the area and then you get into you know your blues and blue is usually going to be something there that's to calm you it wants you to be calm once you know that everything's mellow here and it could also be something there to provide you with guidance and you know could be there hey it wants to be clear and provide good communication. So, I think maybe if you have like a blue orb and like really good evp's in the area that would make a lot of sense because you know it wants to have clear communication with you and so if you see blue orbs maybe go back with an evp to the area and you know see if you can get something that way and then you have extra evidence for a haunting in the area so it could be like hey we're here why aren't you trying to communicate we want to communicate. So, there it could be that is what they're doing I mean blue could be just trying to let off a calming sense of calmness for the area, but it could also be like hey we're here we want to communicate with you if you want to. So, I think it'd be you know interesting to go back to areas that are common with blue orbs and you know try some evp's and other techniques see what other evidence you can gather which that's always a good thing with orbs is if you're wanting to prove that it's a paranormal orb and not a camera trick or a function. If you have other evidence to go along with it that will help and then silver orbs are typically entities that are trapped in that place like they can't leave where they are so they they're going to be strongly associated with that. So that's likely in my opinion to be you know someone who lived there before and doesn't want to leave their possession behind then you get into black orbs, um black typically indicates that the area is unsafe something negative probably happened there in the past so with black orbs if you're getting a lot of those you know it's probably a good idea not to return to the area or to leave the area. That is the spirits warning you hey this is not a good place for you to be get out or it's just simply that the spirit that's there doesn't want you there so it's best to respect that and leave. Gray or smoky looking orbs could be a sign of depression of the spirit that's there or it could be you know the spirit you know recognizing if you're having trouble with depression they may recognize that and they may manifest that way and you know just could be their way hey you know you're dealing with this you want to make sure you know you're dealing with this as well and so you're you know getting a lot of gray orbs in your photographs you know might be a way to look and if you are experiencing that um it might just be the spirit realm trying to get your attention like hey go get help for this and I would strongly recommend you do so if you're struggling with that. And then pink orbs are often messengers of love so they could be you know maybe something very lovingly happened in this area or they're just messengers of love and so that's kind of a basic rundown of the different colors of orbs which there's you know multiple more colors with more meanings behind them and definitely go deeper into these colors but that's just a basic rundown of some of the more common colors. Now when looking to debunk orbs in photographs one of the another thing that is good to look at is the location of the orb because that will tell you more solidly if it is an orb or if it's something else so in photographs reflections won't fall directly behind a person or an object so if it's like behind something and appears to be following from someone like it's directly like it's directly behind them then it's probably an orb because there shouldn't be a reflection there so then also if it's really dense then it's more likely to be an orb. If you've got something that's pretty transparent it more than likely isn't an a true orb it likely is just a bug or some kind of reflection or a dust particle so those are two good things to look at to try and tell if you have an actual orb or something else and so now I'm going to kind of look at orbs outside of photographs there's lots of different theories and different ways they've manifested themselves over the years so being outside of photographs it's kind of weird I haven't found just a whole lot on it in my brief research but what I've gathered is you know you have a lot of folklore regarding like ghost lights know lights that appear at a distance but never get closer or never get further away and never closer they're just kind of out there and there's so many different legends that go out there from miners carrying a light to you know headless specters you know carry on things like that but then there's also other things that kind of lend into some of the picture theories as well such as so we go back to the green orbs being something of nature so one thing that physical orbs outside of pictures could be is a lot of folklore think that it could be you know the elves or fairy folk or you know things like that or you know sprites that are in their travel form. They go into like these little balls of light to travel and that would make sense being of nature because when you think of you know your elves especially you got you know woodland elves and you know you got all these different types of elves usually associated with a different aspect of nature so that could make sense for a green orb to you know actually be a photograph potentially of an elf in travel form. Another thing is you know the will o wisp you know ghost lights as they're called by some now these could be often explained as you know swamp gases which is basically methane and phosphine mixed together and those mix and then you add in oxygen that can cause an internal explosion which gives off you know the light that you see and so that could be a possibility especially if you're in a foggy or swampy area or near a sewer where there's you know that wet area filled with decaying substance that could cause that phenomenon and that makes a lot of sense we think that the sightings of that phenomenon has gone down over the years as a lot of swamp lands have been drained for developmental purposes and so without as much swamp lands around it makes sense that there's been a decline in reports of that type of phenomenon but it's still a possibility and there are still a report to those out there and so again going back to it being you know a fairy or sprite or elf in travel form their habitats being taken away it's likely that you know seeing them in their travel form they're not showing us that much anymore because we're taking away where they're living and so that could be an explanation in that decline. So one more kind of non-picture non-photograph related orb type phenomenon is ball lightning ball lightning is something that has been reported for hundreds of years but it's never until just recently been much understood it's still not very well understood to my understanding but it has recently been recreated in a lab per say and it really does kind of match the description of an orb because it is just little round pieces of light that appear and it actually can be dangerous um I believe it burnt down at church in the 1600s it was a very famous case of the ball lightning and there's different theories on what ball lighting is and so it could be orbs. Most common explanation for ball lightning one explanation comes from Vladimir Torchilin again I probably mispronounced that name really badly but he theorizes that it's not actually true lightning but it's actually light that is trapped inside a bubble or sphere of thin air and since the light's trapped in the air and it's an you know it's a bubble of air it shows itself as you know an orb and then others believe that it could be vaporized ground material that's been pushed upwards by a shock wave and that kind of creates the orbs that are seen for just a few brief seconds and then like I said the ball line that's been recreated in a lab the way that was done was they had electricity they used electricity to vaporize small particles of silicone and when they did that it created spheres of blue orange and white light that lasted for about eight seconds and so yeah wasn't necessarily ball lightning but it was but it creates these spheres so if these right circumstances occur in nature that could be what people are seeing and accounting it to be you know these paranormal spirits or orbs. What is it I don't know that's up to you to figure out in your you know your own journey so if you're looking at pictures and you see something that you think may be an orb maybe yeah you have to look into the photograph further and look for other clues and if it's something that you found during a paranormal investigation look at the evidence outside of the photograph that you also gathered on that investigation that may help you determine if this is truly an orb of the paranormal or simply a malfunction or non-ghostly being in your photo

Yeah so there it is that is a very brief rundown on the orb phenomenon and I hope you all enjoyed it if you have any pictures of orbs that you'd like to share I'd love to see it you can email me at potentpuffin@gmail.com or you can connect with me on Instagram or twitter at potent puffin and you know just you know reference this episode so I know what you're talking about and I'd love to see it or if you have a story about you know seeing some kind of light while you're out that wasn't explained I'd love to hear those stories from you. So yeah, and if you enjoyed you know keep on listening paranormal puffin comes out every third Friday of the month and I'll catch y'all on the next episode I hope everyone you know having a good time on whatever you're doing tonight.

WAMPUS CAT

Hello there and welcome to the Paranormal Puffin a Potent Puffin side show and I'm your host Jake Thomas now this week I'll be discussing a particular cryptid that is often associated with the Appalachian Mountains but has been found as far as the Midwest and into some southern states and it has a very interesting history in my opinion and this creature would be none other than the wampus cat now the wampus cat is interesting to me because it has several kind of origin stories two of them kind of contradict each other in a way. They have some confliction but they also provide some interesting insight to the creature and another interesting fact about the wampus cat that isn't really in the sense of the cat itself but just something interesting about it is the mascot of the high school in my hometown not the high school I went to but the town that I'm from the high school there their mascot is the Wampus Cats that would be Conway High in Conway Arkansas so that's interesting so I kind of grew up near the wampus cat in a sense and my brother went to that high school and so I went to a lot of games and got to see the really cool wampus cat statue that they have and so now let's get into what is the wampus cat.

Now the wampus cat is essentially a cat often described similar to a regular cougar or mountain lion but they have the ability to walk on hind legs like a person and they also are often associated with having the ability to cause a lot of confusion and make a person to like kind of go crazy in a sense and another interesting fact is if you hear their howl it's often been believed that if you hear it howl or wine that means there's going to be a death of some kind in the next three days not necessarily yours but maybe someone around you or just someone in your community it often signifies death within three days so that's interesting and according to some sources it has a very bad odor about it which is pretty common for a lot of cryptids but the particular reason that the wampus cat is believed to have a foul odor is as it's only been seen at night it's believed it only comes out at night and that during the day it lives in sewers. I find that kind of odd because in my mind the wampus cat is more of a being outside kind of cryptid it's not something that I'd initially think of as being something that would be in the sewers but that is one belief so that's pretty interesting and they often are described as being black in appearance like dark jet black sorry Conway High they are not blue usually but they are often described as being black in appearance with yellow eyes.

So given that I'm going to go into some of the common ideas of where the wampus cat came from so first the name kind of comes from the term cattywampus which is depending on where you're from could have a couple different meanings. So cattywampus generally in my mind is describing something that's kind of wonky it's not quite right you know it's like something's off about it it's all cattywampus. It could also mean something that's just been put in a corner so there's that just kind of just in a corner I don't really think I've never thought of that as being cattywampus, cattywampus is usually something that's off and then could also come from describing just an unknown animal that is abnormal or strange that's unidentifiable so for some people cattywampus just means that that's animal is not real it's just unexplained and so over time I could see where that could come into being describing the wampus cat and evolving into want this cat especially since the word catamount which is also similar in pronunciation to cattywampus is a term that describes is used for cougars and lynx and given that these are often found in the Appalachians it's where they're mostly associated with it makes sense because there were cougars there once but their numbers have dwindled I'm not even sure if they're still a wild cougar population or not so that could be where the terms for wampus cat comes from but now for the creature itself.

It's often put into origins from tales of the Cherokee so there's two origins of the wampus cat that are Cherokee involved the first is a Cherokee legend about this demon spirit I believe it's pronounced Ew'ah he was the spirit of madness and this one tribe or one group of Cherokee they had this spirit of madness this demon was feeding on the dreams of the children I believe and that's kind of where it got its powers and this demon if you came in contact with it it had the power to drive you insane and so the elders and the shaman the war chiefs of this tribe they all got together like we got to stop this but we can't just go send all our warriors out to fight this demon we have to do it a different way so they chose their strongest smartest quickest brave his name was I believe Standing Bear or it could be Great Fellow depending on the source but he was basically he's the top dog of the group and they chose him to go fight this demon and so they got him ready he goes out and he's gone for several weeks and his wife running deer is concerned for him because he's gone for so long and eventually Standing Bear comes back but when he comes back he is scratching at his eyes his eyes are gone black and he's like scratching out like he's trying to pull him out and instantly they knew that he had been defeated by Ew'ah this spirit of madness and that he had gone mad himself and because of this condition he was essentially he was legally dead by the Cherokee customs of the day and so he could no longer go about his duties he was eventually he was able to get to where he could pick berries and like gather wheat the kind things of that nature with the young girls and the widows but he was no longer this this dominant brave that he once was. And well Running Deer she is very upset about this she she's sad for her husband and she's wants revenge on this demon for causing her husband to be become like this and to lose his status so she goes to the war chiefs and the shamans and they come up with a plan they're going to allow Running Deer to go and fight this demon herself so they give her a booger mask which is to my understanding it's kind of like it's a mask that represents a demon that they use to like warn off and portray them in different rituals and they give her the head of a bobcat as a mask which according to the legend Ew'ah's one weakness was the spirit of the bobcat so they equipped her with this bobcat mask and then I believe they gave her some kind of like black tar to help mask her scent and so running deer she goes out into the woods and a few days go by and she hasn't found this demon yet and then she notices these strange footprints by a riverbed and then along with these footprints is the breastplate of her husband so she knows that it must be Ew'ah and she goes and she follows these tracks and she finds this this spirit of madness demon and she sneaks up behind it doing her best to remain stealthy and not be seen and then when Ew'ah finally notices he goes to attack her but she presents this bobcat the head of this bobcat to it and when it does the Ew'ah's magic that causes the madness reversed and drove Ew'ah mad and he fell into this pool of water and essentially that was the last of Ew'ah and so then Running Deer she returns to the village and the shaman the war chiefs are all happy the village is now safe the children aren't having their dreams eaten by this demon and supposedly they did something and now Running Deer's spirit has been allowed to fuse with that of the bobcat and she was left to continue roaming the hills to ensure that this demon never returned and that is the wampus cat is Running Deer and it's her out there protecting her village and her people from this demon or any new threats that may come and I really like that story it's an interesting story it you know it shows a lot of stuff to it and it provides a good explanation of the wampus cat it's actually kind of a protector in a way and that could in a since see why the wampus cat attacks some people or takes some you know livestock is because it's these people who weren't on their land before and it sees new settlers or you know people today as encroaching on her ancestral lands and she's going to protect that. Another story that involves the Cherokee is the most common legend I think it's the one I've always heard in regards to the wampus cat and this one is pretty simple this woman she was just didn't want to mind her own business basically so the men of her tribe including her husband they were out on a sacred hunting trip where they shared various stories and secrets and they told things that only the circle of people was supposed to know and she wanted to know what went on during this these hunting trips so she snuck it along and one night while they're at their fire telling their stories and telling these secrets she hides under these pelts of these cougar pelts so she can hear and well she gets caught and so one of the shaman he uses his magic and infuses the cougar pelt to her and she's banished to never be around people again and so she's just wondering and she's you know pretty much a hybrid human cougar now and so that would explain why she's able to walk on her hind legs and I find that interesting because it pretty much contrast with the other story of Running Deer because in that story the man kind of fell and the woman came in and she was the savior and this story it's the opposite it kind of reinforces certain stereotypes that we have in our culture where the woman was out of her place and the man kind of punished her for that and so there are two there's a lot of underlying differences there but they both provide interesting sights on the wampus cat and what it is and some sources even state that the woman who was fused with the bobcat pelts as the punishment state that she is actually what became Ew'ah so I find that kind of interesting yet that story from my research didn't come about until much later in time so I don't know but I think the story of Running Deer is more likely the true origin of the wampus cat and another origin of the wampus cat that I have heard is that it is a witch who lives in the woods and she transforms herself into a cat into like a mountain lion or cougar in order to steal chicken and poultry or whatever livestock might be around so that she has food to eat and so that kind of is interesting that most the stories of the wampus cat and how it came to be are all come from women becoming this creature in some way whether it be in the role of protector or as punishment or they're just a witch and they want to eat and so that's how they get their food but nonetheless it is a very terrifying thing to come across in the woods as it can cause you to kind of go insane it can oh I kind of forgot what I'm saying there for a second and it can you know walk like a person so it could confuse you what you're saying at first and that could be another reason why it makes you go insane because it confuses you with what you're seeing you might see a cougar walking or a mountain lion walking on its hind legs and it might confuse you and that could set off some of the hysteria and then two if you hear it it's you know noise it could signify that there's going to be a death and that alone is pretty scary and so that's interesting now going back to the physical appearance of the wampus cat it's often said to have you know the general size of a regular cougar mountain lion with the ability to stand on his hind legs and the coloring can range from being jet black like I mentioned before to being similar to that of just a normal cougar mountain lion but another distinguishing feature of the wampus cat depending on source and I don't know where this started but this is kind of the version that Conway High takes and I've seen for a while I thought it was just something that Conway High did to create a more unique mascot but as I've looked into the wampus cat more I've seen other sources that have it like this as well and it's the fact that the wampus cat has six legs now the purpose of having six legs according to Conway High again is there's four to run and two to fight with all its might which makes sense you know you can bat stuff away while it's trying to move more quickly but when you think about these origins of it whether it's the Cherokee woman who's been fused with the pelts or the spirit of running deer it would seem that that could be why there's six legs because once it fuses she has the bobcat legs along with her regular human arms potentially and then the bobcat hind legs fuse with the human legs and there's six legs right there that could put I think it makes sense to me that that's why it has six legs and it goes along with the origin makes sense but I just think that's interesting so that could that's yeah that's kind of the wampus cat and I'm just going to go real briefly over a few other kind of cryptids that kind of fit along with the wampus cat a little bit not too much but one is the Ozark Howler which is kind of like described as being like a bear dog cat with horns and that's found in Oklahoma Missouri and um I think parts of Tennessee maybe but really just this little area of the Ozarks and it's kind of interesting because sometimes it's described as being and it's howl is also associated with death so it makes sense to me that maybe they are one of the same and just because of regional variances there's been a difference and so that would be why it's still you know kind of like feline in some ways but not in others it has other features that separate it but I think they could be coming from similar or origins so I think that's interesting that's one that I need to do more research on myself it's weird because I grew up uh kind of like the foothills of the Ozarks but I don't know much about the Ozark Howler itself and so yeah I'm going to do more research on that one so that'll be interesting that'll be fun and that's all I really got for this week and yeah I hope you all enjoyed if you did you know give me a subscribe follow you know do all that check out the potent puffin as well and I'll be getting a write up on the wampus cat up on to the potent puffin blog pretty soon if I haven't already by the time this releases but look looking forward to that and if you feel a good mood uh give me a review or leave a comment something and let me know what you think and I'll catch you all on the next episode of Paranormal Puffin coming out every third Friday of the month.

FYVIE CASTLE

Hello there and welcome to the Paranormal Puffin a Potent Puffin side show and I'm your host Jake Thomas and sitting here beside me is Kita the spooky elk hound now this week's or this month's episode I'll be discussing something that is kind of cool and kind of creepy a really cool haunted location that I first discovered after falling asleep on my recliner and waking up to one of those ghost finding shows on the history channel discovery channel maybe the travel channel I don't remember but we're gonna have to go across the big pond here this month and head over to Scotland for this location but I will be discussing Fyvie Castle. Fyvie Castle is a really interesting place it goes back to the 13th century when it was originally built I believe by William the Lion and it's been owned by several different families or clans over the centuries it's been owned by the Preston's, the Meldrum's, the Seton's the Gordons and the Leith's and I believe it is now currently owned by the National Trust of Scotland. I believe but it's interesting because it kind of has paranormal supernatural ties in multiple ways it has been cursed kind of and it also has hauntings. So I'll first discuss the curse that kind of came upon it which is attributed to Thomas the Rhymer or True Thomas who is an interesting character himself he was kind of a prophet if you would say in the 13th century and at one point he was taken by the Queen of Elfland to the land of the fairies and he lived there for I believe seven years and then when he returned he was gifted with the gift of prophecy and being unable to tell a lie and so one day this Thomas the Rhymer he was approaching Fyvie Castle and I'll go back up real fast I've forgot one kind of interesting thing about his prophecies so he actually one of the main prophecies that he was attributed to was he predicted the death of Alexander II in

1286 he said "on tomorrow before noon shall blow the greatest wind ever was heard before in Scotland" and the Earl of Dunbar who he told this to didn't believe it because the next day around the ninth hour he's like the weather hasn't changed it's not going to be the worst wind we've ever heard and so he sent for Thomas the Rhymer and then at noon they got word that Alexander II had died and that really shook up things in Scotland at the time. So his prophecy did come true it just didn't come true quite in the literal sense that this Earl of Dunbar was expecting. So, anyways now fast forward back to the story he was coming up on Fyvie Castle I believe he was expected there for seven years and a day before he finally arrived and then when he finally arrived it was like a big storm going around but where Thomas was like his immediate person was unaffected by the storm and so when he approached the castle gate the wind blew it shut and he took this you know not very nicely he was really offended by this and so he said

" Fyvie Fyvie thou'se never thrive as long as there in three stones there's one in the oldest tower there's one in the lady's bower there's one in the water gate and there three stones you never get" and basically he was just saying that there's these three stones I believe they're taken from some church grounds when the castle was built and he's like until you find these three stones you know the castle the people who owned the castle will never thrive a lot of people say that means that it will never follow a direct succession to the eldest son which has never happened since this occurred.

So, it's kind of been kind of cursed like that and I believe there's been two of the stones have been found there's one that they say is built into the foundation of Preston tower which is the oldest tower and then they found one in the charter room which is the lady's bower and that one is on display I believe and this is kind of where they get the name the weeping stones is because it said that these stones whenever anything around them is wet they'll be dry and whenever everything around them is dry they'll be wet and the one that's on display kind of shows that tendency and then the third one has not been found I believe it's speculated that it's in the Ythan River I believe it's called . So, that's interesting and another thing that's been kind of attributed to this curse I haven't been found as much information about it but I guess there's a secret chamber that it said if it were to be opened it would bring the death of the laird and bring blindness to their wife and according to my readings it's been open twice and each time the laird of the castle died and one of their wives went completely blind and one of their wives had vision problems the rest of their life but that's all I could find I couldn't find out which lairds it was or when those openings happened. So, I don't know just how factual those events are they're not as concrete in my mind as the weeping stones and the falling into secession to the next son stuff. So that was really cool that's kind of you know Thomas the Rhymer's involvement at Fyvie. So, that's interesting that I find that really cool because you got this kind of guy who has a history of you know telling these cool prophecies he's got a lot of things attributed to him and he's kind of put a curse on this place and it hasn't been broken yet and then on top of that Fyvie is also considered one of the most haunted places in Scotland. I believe it's said there's a total of nine ghosts that live there but there's about four that are like the main ghost and I'll go over them now.

So I guess the big ghost that is around Fyvie is known as the Green Lady and it's believed that the Green Lady is Dame Lilias Drummond and she was the wife of Alexander Seton and they had five daughters together which kind of goes back to the Thomas the Rhymer curse they've had five daughters so you can't succeed to the firstborn son if there are no sons and so Alexander Seton he's getting frustrated with this and he wants to have a son and so he started to have a relationship with Lilias's cousin Grizel Leslie trying to have a son with her and stories kind of differentiate here some people say that he began keeping Lilias locked away and starving her so that he could have this affair to have a son and then when her family tried to rescue her he had them all killed in front of her and I believe they say the room that a lot of that occurred it's now called the murder room and then some say that she just retired to her family's home at Fife but then they kind of join together and say that she did eventually go to Fife and that is where she died and then shortly after she died at her family's home in Fife, Alexander Seton and Grizel Leslie they got married and on their wedding night they went to their chambers which was in a tower that was and the room I believe was 50 feet in the air off the ground from ground level and they kept hearing a howling noise outside the window. They're having just a lot of disturbance in the night and first they kind of just attribute it to being the wind and just natural stuff but then eventually they checked out the window and they found carved into the stone on the windowsill D Lilias Drummond and ever since there's kind of been this presence of this green lady and they attribute her as being one of the main hauntings of the castle and it's also said that she leaves behind the scent of rose petals and she often wanders to castle bemoaning about the betrayal of her husband and so it's kind of interesting they say that when she returned to fight the reason of her death because she was really young she was just so heartbroken over these events and that is what actually killed her and now she haunts the castle and I guess according to some mediums who have been there they say that she is considered the head ghost she rules over the other ghosts in the castle.

Then there's a second lady who has haunted the castle in the past and she is known as the Gray Lady they believe that she is Lady Meldrum and before she died she apparently requested to be buried in a secret chamber within the castle and then in 1920 there is some reason the castle's gun room had to be renovated or something and so they had to open this secret chamber that they didn't know about and in the walls they found a skeleton and so they thought they were going to be respectful and give it a proper burial in the cemetery on the grounds well after they did that they started seeing you know apparitions that are having increased hauntings by this supposed Gray Lady and then when they realized that this was all going on and when it started they decided to move those remains back into that area of the castle and had it sealed back up and after that the sightings of this Gray Lady have seized. So it's kind of like she wanted this one thing and she got it and she's at peace and then they disrupted her you know her body and she came back and made it known that she was not happy about that even though the people thought they were being respectful they kind of did the opposite of what this person wanted and they got it fixed and she's kind of left the place in peace again.

Then a third ghost that lives there is known as the phantom trumpeter he's got kind of an interesting story behind him. They believe it's the ghost of a man named Andrew Lammie and supposedly he died of a broken heart when he found out about the death of this woman that he had loved named Agnes. They say that the phantom trumpeter he'll often be seen dressed in rich tartans. He'll appear and when approached he disappears and they say that the sound of this trumpet kind of could mean the death of someone coming up and at first that's kind of all I found about him was that little description but then I did a little more digging and I found out that he lived in the 18th century and I can't really read my notes I believe it was the laird of the castle at the time they both fancied the same woman this Agnes lady and so they took this Andrew Lammie and he got sold into slavery and sent to the West Indies and at some point he was able to escape or buy his freedom I'm not real sure but he returned to Scotland returned to Fyvie Castle and when he returned he had found out that Agnes had died and he was just so heartbroken that he died over the news of this. So, then they say that before he died he swore that he would have his revenge on the laird for you know having him sent into slavery and not being able to be with the woman that he loved because he was jealous of their relationship and so that's kind of why they say that the sound of his trumpet could signify the death of the current laird of the castle.

Then there's a little girl named Annie who can be seen in the stairwells often and supposedly she enjoys having people visit the castle they say that people that have reached out to her say that Annie says she likes having people there she enjoys you know having people to play with like she enjoys being able to share the space with people and she's just an innocent little girl and now the final ghost that they have that haunts Fyvie his name is John Pollock and apparently he's the only ghost in the castle that can be harmful they say that he stays in the library which is where the mask that they had on him when he was hung is on display and he was hung for murder. So, he was a violent man apparently in this life and he continues those violent tendencies in the next, but they say that the Green Lady as she is the head ghost, she prevents him from doing harm to anybody in the castle but he does wish to do hard to people. I guess there's been reports of people who are more sensitive to spirits and stuff they say that they go to the library they get nauseous and can't stay in there because just this strong negativity that this John Pollock puts out. But like I said the Green Lady doesn't allow him to do hard because she's the head ghost apparently and I just find that just really kind of crazy that this one there's just this one malicious spirit there but he's not able to actually do harm. So, I guess that's a good thing for the Green Lady but that's really kind of interesting and those are all like the major ghosts. I know I said there's about nine that are known I think I covered about five or six but those are the only ones that I could really find any substantial information about them.

But yeah so, it's Fyvie Castle it's somewhere I've always wanted to visit. I hope someday I will get to and yeah I just I just really think the whole head ghost thing is cool I've never heard about that until researching Fyvie Castle so I find that kind of interesting that there's a head ghost for the location they kind of you know keep the other spirits in check that's really an interesting concept I'm going to look more into and see if that's a common thing in places that have more than one haunting and yeah that's really all I got. If you have any cool stories about Fyvie if you've ever visited Fyvie or had any encounters there, I'd love to hear about them you know you can leave a review and mention it or send me an email at potentpuffin@gmail.com send me a message on twitter or something let me know your experiences with Fyvie. I really love to hear about them or if you're watching on YouTube throw down a comment you know tell me what you know about Fyvie I'd love to hear about it and so yeah I look forward to doing some research for the next Paranormal Puffin for June and I hope you all enjoyed this and stay spooky y'all enjoy what you enjoy and I'll catch you all in the next episode.

SUPERSTITIOUS WHISTLE

Hello there and welcome to the Paranormal Puffin a Potent Puffin sideshow and I'm your host Jake Thomas and sitting here beside me is Kita the elkhound now it's been a few months since I've had a new episode of Paranormal Puffin and I'm excited to be back at it and this month's episode kind of comes a little close because I get my inspiration from talking with one of my co-workers here we don't work with each other often because we're on different shifts but occasionally with shift coverage we get to work together and we always have these discussions about the paranormal and different folklore and cryptids and things of that nature and it's always makes those shifts go by pretty fast because we get on these little talks and it's always fun and one thing we always do is we always share with each other you know strange experiences that we have with each other like a few weeks ago I had this incident with my light where the light fixture just fell but the retaining screws were still all the way in like I had to undo the retaining screws to get the fixture to go back in. So I just thought it was weird because it's like it just fell without this retaining screws being moved and it's kind of a freaky thing but it's something I shared with him because I know we both enjoy those kinds of topics and we when we do this we always talk about things that we know about the topic things similar experiences with either ourselves or someone we know and sometimes if you know like a local legend per se pertaining to the subject will tell it and he shared with me an interesting story the other day. I don't remember the exactly how it went I'll have to ask him again to get the exact story but basically the gist of the story was he was at home and he was getting ready for bed and his wife was outside with their dogs and he heard this very distinct loud whistle like he thought there was someone in the room with him making this whistle but obviously there wasn't he was alone and when his wife came in she asked him if he had been whistling at her because she had heard it too and thought it sounded like it was really close and like they didn't see anyone going by there's like no footprints like he walked up to the road there's like no footprints around and like I said his wife was out with the dogs their dogs are the type that would generally bark if something was around and they were quite they were completely unfazed by these two whistles that they heard

and so it's kind of it like though there's these whistles but don't know the source and so we kind of talked a little bit and as we talked I got to realize like you know there's a lot of superstitions and paranormal based on whistles a lot of folklore a lot of legends based on whistles and so I did a little bit of research if you would say into some of these and I'm going to talk a little bit here about those. You know I was in the Coast Guard and as a sailor I grew to be pretty superstitious even more so than I already was and one of the big superstitions was for sailors is I was always told you never whistle on the bridge and some people will say you don't whistle on a ship at all. The reasoning behind that is you will whistle up a storm and the first time I heard about this I experienced that it is definitely true. So the first time I heard about not whistling on the bridge was I was on watch one night and where I had this chief boatswain's mate who was very old school really cool dude like he could do all the whole navigation by stars like he didn't trust equipment like he was very old school and he was really superstitious he was he was pretty hard dude but he was great guy but anyways we had this break-in who was I was training to do the helm and this kid started whistling that chief kicked him off the bridge like he wasn't allowed to stay on watch because he started to whistle and I asked the chief you know after that kid got sent off the bridge I was like what's up with that and he told me he's like well you'll whistle up a storm and I was like huh okay whatever oh then out about an hour later we got into a pretty good little storm didn't last all night but it was unexpected weather that we weren't anticipating and we got rocked around pretty good for a little while and another time one of the worst storms I can remember in December of 2012 well there's an oil rig that lost its power that it's there's an oil rig and it's tug lost power and we had to go and help with this situation but anyways again someone started whistling on the bridge before we got word of that situation and as we were having to transit to this we got caught up in a horrible storm like it was like 50 knot winds and like 35 foot seas and we got to get pushed around pretty well up there in the Gulf of Alaska but the storm kind of came after someone was whistling on the bridge and so I just find that very strange. I kind of like wonder like well why is that? Well you know some people say well that superstition probably got started because someone found whistling annoying and they didn't want someone annoying them and so they said no whistling on the ship and they made up a reason but there's another reason too and I think it's more accurate because I've seen it I've seen this and they say that it's because when you do that is you're challenging the wind and well you know you challenge nature and it's going to show you what it can do. But something else I kind of learned and just my little bit of light reading and internet searching, and I learned about this thing transcendental whistling came from Asia. I guess the best transcendental whistlers were around in the third century but essentially, it's like I guess this can be used with like yoga but it's a way of controlling your breath usually like long drawn and like resonating like whistling kind of sounds and these people who practice this were able to summon animals they could communicate with spirits, and they could even control the weather. There was one person who I read about he was trying to cross this river and the ferry refused some service and so he laid down a mat and he started practicing this transcendental whistling and the wind came and picked up his mat and carried him over the river. I thought that was pretty interesting but then it kind of makes me think well if they were doing this by whistling and you think about how whistling's you know is challenging the wind what if that's because like a subconscious way when you're whistling on a ship, you're in a way doing this transcendental whistling but you don't know it. You're not doing it properly and so it's triggering this bad weather I don't know it seems like it could be a thought but I don't know.

Then the other big thing that I've always known about with whistling is I've always been told you don't whistle inside because it could summon evil spirits it invites them into the residence where you're at and I've had a little bit experience with this myself and I'll tell you about this so a couple years ago my mom and step-dad they moved into a new house and my wife and I went to go visit them and they'd only been in this house a couple months at this time and we usually stay with them when we go to visit and the first night yeah I think it was like the first or second night we were there my stepdad was whistling I was just walking through the house and my wife repeatedly asked him to stop and after about the third time like she asked him to stop he's like what's the big deal I don't understand why you keep asking me to stop whistling inside the house and so she told him she's like you're going to invite evil spirits in here and he kind of joked it off and didn't think anything of it. Well that night my wife and myself my son were in our room and we're asleep so my son still slept with us in our bed at the time and so he's in there and I don't remember if he spilled his drink or if he wet the bed but something happened and the bed got wet and so we didn't want to sleep in the bed with it being wet. So we went and slept in the living room on the couch for the evening and well that whole night like I wasn't able to go back to sleep and like I couldn't really it was almost like a night of the sleep paralysis almost kind of like I could move but I didn't like really want to I was nervous to move and like I'd look around but like I just felt like this really like heavy presence like I felt like something was like floating above me but I couldn't quite see it but like I could really feel it and it kept me like really nervous and I didn't want to like get up or move around and like I look over and my son was sleeping and so that was good and I thought my wife was asleep she looked like she was asleep to me but then the next morning she said the same thing to me she would experience a pretty similar presence like it didn't feel good like whatever it was it didn't seem friendly to us but it was just strange because she said when she would look over at me it looked like I was asleep and so I thought that was just kind of weird that we had that experience and it was after you know my step dad was whistling in the house and we told him not to do that and so that's just kind of weird and like ever since then going around that house has been kind of kind of strange for me. But I got to thinking that's one of the common things is that like whistling can attract various things and like I already said you know to sum it summons evil spirits into the house if you're whistling indoors but there's other like times and places that whistling can be attracting something unwanted and a few of those are you know at night it disturbs the peace and invites danger which kind of goes along with whistling indoors kind of similar it invites something unwanted and then one that I found really interesting was in Mexico there's this creature called the lechuza I'm not sure i'm saying that entirely correct so forgive me I'm mispronouncing that and you know what but the lechuza is this witch who can turn into an owl and at night she'll whistle and that's how you know she's there because she'll whistle and if you whistle back then it alerts her that you know she's there and that's what she's going to take you away and so she's like this owl lady she's like seven foot tall with a wingspan of 15 foot and she could pick up grown men but she was a witch who got exposed for witchcraft and the townspeople killed her and then she came back as this owl lady. It's just kind of cool I just find it very interesting because it's an interesting creature I want to learn a little more about it but the lechuza is kind of interesting but she kind of does her thing through whistling like if you hear the whistle and you whistle back, she'll come so be careful if you're responding to a whistle.

In like some middle eastern cultures whistling can attract the jinn which are kind of like genies that they bring about misfortune so that's you know you don't want to invite those guys either. in Hawaii some believe that whistling could bring about the night watchers could also bring about the menhune which are like these forest dwarfs but both of those are you know I had some hard time finding exactly why it's bad but like the night watchers I mean you don't want to cross paths with but if you do you know try and show respect for it because they're just they're just doing their thing and try to protect their ancient spirits so just show those guys respect. But then you get to some of the Native Americans and that's where some really interesting things come about in my mind. So according to some Inuit legends and I didn't know od this one myself but my wife she did and she kind of laughed when I told her about it because she was like you didn't know this but apparently if you whistle you're not supposed to whistle under the northern lights so apparently if you whistle at the northern lights the spirits of the lights will carry you away with them so if you don't want to get carried away with the spirits don't whistle at the under the northern lights so keep that in mind if you're ever around them. Then the other one is it kind of this one kind of varies from region to region but it's kind of prevalent in different indigenous people across America and Canada but it's the stick people or the stick Indians. So, the stick Indians they pretty much communicate by whistles. Some say they're forest spirits, and they can vary from being bigfoot like creatures to being dwarfs and some say they're pretty human-like but however they get interpreted they aren't good like you don't want them around. Most tribes like they won't even acknowledge their actual name I could think of a creature around here for the native Alutiiq people and I'm not going to talk about what they're called because my wife would be very upset if I mentioned it. In our house that's kind of how off topic these guys are but and I don't know those guys that my wife just won't let me mention they could be a variation of the stick Indians I'm not 100% sure but that's kind of how they are like that's why they're called stick Indians they won't mention that like the native people won't even mention their true names but that's kind of what they that's one way they communicate it's by whistling and some say that they do it to cause confusion amongst the people they're around or it could just be saying who will whistle back and acknowledge them so that they can come after you and yeah and so what these sick people they sticking is they have some unique powers kind of because some people say that they can cause paralysis and they can hypnotize people and they could caught they could even cause some people to go insane which is just so you're seeing that they can do these things you see why they're bad you don't want to get around them. So if you're you know alone at night and you hear someone whistling at you it might be a good idea not to whistle back because it could be one of these stick Indians and here's a kind of cool thing about them that I kind of put together but is that they communicate by whistling and some say that they can't actually talk but all they could do is mimic birds and that's kind of why they whistle it's because that's kind of how birds do they chirp and whistle but I find that interesting because according to some they're very bigfoot like creatures and my friend who had the whistling experience I was telling about earlier he's always kind of told me that some people within the bigfoot community believe that that's how different bigfoots or sasquatches communicate is by mimicking birds and they some people know this because they'll be in an area they here a bird that doesn't exist there and they'll be it'll be people who are out in known bigfoot territory try to document bigfoots they'll hear these series of chirps from birds that aren't native to that area and shouldn't be in that area so they think that these bigfoot maybe learn these bird sounds and migrated. So, I just find that interesting and you know that there's that bigfoot connection with these all these stick Indians are they the same maybe, maybe not. I don't think so because bigfoots could can be malicious but they're not always, but these stick Indians they generally are malicious and so I think that could be two similar things that might get confused but I don't know for sure and that's pretty much all I have for the whistling so kind of neat little topic to listen to and think about and I would just suggest you know if you're alone at night and you don't want to attract anything unwanted don't whistle and don't whistle indoors or on a ship. So yeah that's what I have for this week I hope you all enjoyed it and I hope to be getting back to monthly episodes of Paranormal Puffin and be sure to also check out the Potent Puffin Podcast as well and if you enjoyed you know give a like leave a review comment whatever follow me on twitter and instagram at potent puffin uh like my facebook page if you want to and yeah I'll catch you all next time and take care all.

THE PHILADELPHIA EXPERIMENT

Hello there and welcome to the Paranormal Puffin a Potent Puffin side show and I'm your host Jake Thomas and sitting here beside me is Kita the elkhound. Has the U.S. government conducted experiments involving time travel, teleportation, and invisibility it's likely whether these all are conducted within a single experiment that's what is suggested by taking a look at the Philadelphia Experiment at the USS Eldridge now basically the story of what happened with the USS Eldridge is that it October 28th of 1943 the vessel was at the Philadelphia naval shipyard and while docked there it disappeared it supposedly it reappeared at Norfolk Virginia at the naval shipyard there then shortly after being spotted it disappeared it reappeared in Philadelphia shipyard once again and supposedly the time onboard the vessel was now 10 minutes prior to when it initially disappeared from Philadelphia and that's basically the gist of what happened. They say that so crew members began getting this mysterious illness became very ill some became fused to the vessel inside the bulkheads from side effects of the teleportation by going from one deck to another and some went like it said began developing mental illnesses and largely for the next several years it was not really mentioned and they say this could be for a government brainwashing of the sailors it wasn't really until the mid 50s that it started becoming known kind of that this was a thing and that became about because Morris Jessup began receiving these letters from a Carl Allen also known as Carlos Miguel Allende they corresponded through letters about things such as ufo technology and how ufos and alien technology works and how they interact.

Jessup he authored a book called what was it "The Case for UFO's" and shortly after that book was published in 1955 in 1956 a mysterious copy of the book ended up at the office of naval research and this copy of the book was unique as it had annotations written inside it. It appeared to be from three different people but further inquiry from the ONR and Morris Jessup they believe that these three annotations were all by this Carl Allen, Carlos Allende guy.They believe this is the same guy based on the previous letters that he had corresponded with Jessup but these annotations made it look like it was a conversation between three people one of which may have been an extraterrestrial but in these annotations they mentioned this so-called Philadelphia Experiment and with that there are two ONR officers who became obsessed with the idea of this ship that had teleported from one place to another. And after that they had the annotations added to the book basically, they made a new copy of the book with the annotations printed within and they used a military contractor Varo Publishing I believe or something like that and they published 127 copies of this of this this version of the book and with that it kind of spread the rumor of this experiment.

It essentially this Carl Allende what he described as he was aboard this merchant vessel the Andrew Furuseth, I believe it was and what he said he saw is he was at the Philadelphia naval shipyard and this green bluish glow came about the Eldridge and then it disappeared and allegedly people in Norfolk saw it there that day and then it was back in Philadelphia.

Now some easy debunks on this is there's inner inlet canals that are off use to civilian use and these canals could make a two-day trip from Philadelphia to Norfolk possible within six hours so that could explain why someone may be like oh the Eldridge was here then it wasn't and now it's back again there in Norfolk that could explain the quickness of the transition there.

Then another thing is there were experiments being conducted by the military in Philadelphia but they were not anything that would cause teleportation simply they were conducting experiments with generators using higher frequency generators they wanted to see how they would affect the ship and a lot of times with the Philadelphia experiment you'll hear about the degaussing equipment to create invisibility and that a side effect of becoming invisible was the teleportation but the degaussing equipment yes it was equipped with the degaussing equipment as was the what was it I forget there was another ship that was docked alongside it they both received the degaussing equipment but all that really does is it did create invisibility in a sense but not visually what it did is creates electromagnetic interference so that it would prevent torpedoes from u-boats that use electromagnetics to find their target for being able to find the Eldridge. So that's kind of what that is between the degaussing equipment and the generator experiments it's possible that it could have created some kind of after effect that made a glowing that this guy could have saw.

But what's kind of odd is for me is looking back at some of the ship's logs or what's reported to have been the ship's logs is the Eldridge was never in Philadelphia or Norfolk in October of 1943. It was mostly in New York and in September of 43 it conducted sea trials in Bahamas and around Bermuda so it likely went through the Bermuda triangle so I kind of wonder if maybe that had something to do with it because it's just where to be Bermuda triangle anyways it's maybe some kind of after effect of being there mixed with these electromagnetic testings for the degaussing may have caused something.

But see yeah so that's kind of how that is so it may have teleported may not have but here's where things get really kind of weird and go in another direction.

Other than this Morris Jessup and Carl Allen, Carlos Allende however he wants to be recognized go about saying this teleportation, invisibility experiment is there is another guy who makes reports of this Philadelphia experiment at his personal experience with it and it gets really weird so there's this guy Al Bieleck, I'm not real sure how you pronounce it but he claims that he was a sailor on the Eldridge but what it was the Eldridge he wasn't Al Bielek he was Edward Cameron and his brother Duncan Cameron was also a sailor aboard the Eldridge. Now Mr, Bielik, he claims that growing up he had knowledge of things that he didn't know how he knew and he saw in 1988 the film the Philadelphia experiment and he said upon watching the film he started having flashbacks to being on the boat and he sought out psychics to help him understand why he was having this deja vu feeling when he watched the film and why he was having all these flashbacks and he had uncovered that he was actually this Edward Cameron and that he had he was there the day that the experiment allegedly took place and while the ship was teleporting he felt sick but his brother jumped overboard and got lost in time it apparently he regained consciousness in the year 2137 he was in a hospital with radioactive burns which one of the reports is that all the sailors who were there had burn marks on them. So, afterwards he was there for only a couple of weeks at 2137 but he then traveled to 2749 and spent two years there and he describes you know what the future was like as but eventually he basically became like a time travel agent for the government and he went on a mission to 1983 where he was then you know briefed on his time travel and what was going on and at some point in all this the government became distrusting of him and so they sent him on missions instead of going forward in time he was continually going back in time until the year he was born and the idea with that is that he would just disappear once he went so far to the past that he wasn't born that he would just disappear and he states that that is what he was reborn into this identity of Al.

With that but with the regressing back it did alternate brainwashing as he was going through these time travel experiments, he had that memory kind of hidden from him and it wasn't until he watched the film that it brought those back forth that he knew what had happened.

So, I just really find that interesting that he thinks that he claims that he had traveled all this time and then it's just kind of interesting I think and so I always found the Philadelphia experiment interesting concept the it really kind of ties in a lot of different things from time travel to teleportation, invisibility, government testing and what really happened and I don't know if we'll ever know what really happened highly likely this is all just a fabricated story by Carl Allende that other people have found ways to make their mark with it but it is interesting because it comes from a weird time and just the fact that the office of naval research really kind of took off with you know reprinting copies of Jessup's book with those annotations that they took like the two officers like really took personal interest in this experiment and it kind of makes me wonder why like why did they take such an interest in this book to have it republished with these annotations why was the office of naval research really digging into this like how come they didn't just dismiss it like this is some crazy guy like why did they go with it and so much I don't understand I just feel like if it was nothing then they would have just disregarded even receiving that copy of the book but they really wanted to try to figure out where this book came from who was writing the stuff in it and even republished it with that.

So, it's kind of I just find that odd because I feel like someone like somewhere like the office of naval research would have just brushed it along the side and not even paid any attention to receiving the book in the first place so that's kind of weird for me but yeah.

that's really all I have of the Philadelphia experiment I really want to look forward to how the Bermuda triangle may have worked into this because I feel like that could have like maybe they had some kind of delayed response for being there and upon these experiments it may have been simple just trying to find a way to elude torpedoes and just simple degaussing gone wrong I don't know but it's very interesting but those are really the only two people I could find that really had any experience with the Philadelphia experiment and claims to what it was and what happened is Morris Jessup an Carl Allende's interaction with Jessup's book as well as Alfred Bielek at his supposed time traveling from the experiment so that's just kind of interesting food for thought but yeah but like I said like these people saying they saw it in Philadelphia but according to ship's logs it was never in Philadelphia or Norfolk according to port logs the SS Andrew Furuseth that Allende was supposedly on watching this it wasn't at either place at that time it was on a convoy had left just a few days prior to the alleged events so maybe some logs were doctored to make it appear that no one was where they allegedly were I don't know but it's kind of interesting and I've always been intrigued by the Philadelphia experiment and the USS Eldridge and just wanted to know what really went on did it travel through time did it travel from one place to another it during that teleportation it created a break in time for somebody I don't know that we never will most likely.

That it created invisibility likely not but it's interesting because you know they say that Nikola Tesla was involved in making some coils for the for the equipment that they put on there, uh there's a lot of talk about Einstein's unified field theory being mixed with alien technology for the government and that's what led up to some to this experiment is using a technology to test the unified field theory that created an extra plane that was needed to create the invisibility and that's what they were trying to achieve was finding that fourth plane of reality or whatever that's allowed to you know see all dimensions at once or something I don't know but it's just an interesting little tidbit I hope to find more research on it go a little deeper myself but yeah that's about it for the Philadelphia experiment a little quick short episode today and I hope to see you all next month and if you want to just learn a little more about me in my daily life check out the Potent Puffin podcast as well and check me out on YouTube, I got some cool stuff going on there and catch you all next time.

MOOSHAM CASTLE:
Witches, Werewolves, and Ghosts!

Hello there and welcome to the Paranormal Puffin a Potent Puffin sideshow and I'm your host Jake Thomas and sitting here beside me is Kita the elkhound today they're talking about a cool place in Austria that I recently learned about, and I want to choose to do somewhere in Austria because back in February I noticed that this podcast ranked uh up in the top 80 of documentary podcast on apple charts in Austria so I wanted to give a little shout out to whoever's listening to this podcast in Austria say hey I know you're out there and I want to thank you for listening to my show. So I decided to do some research and find some cool haunted place in Austria to learn about and share with everyone and so the place that I found and was really intrigued with is Moosham Castle it's in Salzburg Austria I believe is how you say it and it's got a really cool history behind it a lot of paranormal stuff going on there from ghosts to witches to werewolves it's got everything. So, I saw that I was like I got to learn more about this place, and it is definitely a cool place cool history and I hope to someday get to visit it. It has entered my list of cool haunted places I want to visit someday and so without any more I'm going to get to it and share with everyone what I learned about Moosham Castle this past week. So it's a an old place obviously and before it became a castle it was previously a Roman fortress that by the time the castle came along was no longer there but the same grounds the castle got built on around 1191 is the first like real documentation of the castle being there and after that in around 1285 it was seized by the Prince Archbishop of Salzburg and it saw a lot of war during its early years as there was the Austrian Hungarian wars the Flemish revolt against uh Maximilian um German Peasant wars so a lot of battles a lot of wars fought on the grounds of this castle and near the castle so right there off the bat you got you know a lot of death associated with it because of the wars and the battles so that kind of you know gives it the grounds to have you know a haunting but you go in past that and there's so much more other than just war other tragedies other you know paranormal activity going around that sets this place up to be a prime haunted location and the major thing that surrounds this castle is the Salzburg witch trials also known as the I'm trying to say this properly the Zaubererjackal trials it was a 15-year witch hunt basically from 1675 to 1690 and there was around 139 people that got executed and from the result of being accused of being witches and the unique thing about this witch hunt in my mind is a lot of the people who are accused and executed were actually male and they were young like teenage young adult men is who were the primary target to this particular witch hunt and those who were accused of being witches they were tortured a lot before they were finally sentenced to death eventually a lot were had their hands cut off and were branded often paraded through town as a warning and then once they finally confessed they were given slow deaths but eventually a lot were burned. I believe and it was a huge range of ages in this the youngest recorded person was a young man who was about 10 years old and the oldest was this old woman Margaret I believe her name was and she was 80 by the time that she was executed. But a lot of them were like teenage just under 21 year old men but the one thing that they really had in common is a lot of them came from the lower class they were beggars they lived in the slums they were generally societal outcasts and that could be they used the witch hunt as like an excuse to kind of purge them from society almost but it's got an interesting history for the witch hunt and how it got started essentially you know before 1600 in Austria there wasn't much going on in the you know accusing people being witches and getting all upset about it but then in 1611 1613 um a new archbishop came around I believe and he made a bunch of like anti-witchcraft laws and they really caught on so by the time that these witch trials started in Salzburg at Moosham Castle it really gave a lot of grounds to you know pick these people out and really torture them and get them to you know get the point where they could execute them simply for being accused of being a witch and with them being in the lower class like I said they didn't really have much credit to their name. So no one's really vouched for them and it was just you know no one's saying you're not so confess and this really got started in about 1675 a lady named Barbara Koller she got accused of being a witch after she demanded alms from an innkeeper and when he refused she allegedly put a curse on him and she got arrested for being a thief and for being a witch and she has been tortured to you know basically confess that she's a witch and during that she admitted that her son Paul Jacob Koller was a sorcerer himself and had made a pact with the devil and so the authorities really took that and ran with it and her partner at the time not Jacob's dad but just the guy she was with at the time he confirmed he's like yeah this is true Jacob's you know in with the devil and he does magic and so they really started looking hard for him for a couple of years and they never really caught up to him. He kind of started becoming a legend as you know they weren't catching him and so his name was kind of becoming popular especially among the lower class he kind of became somewhat of a folk hero to them and after I think about two years of looking for him they received word that he had died but then after they found out that he had allegedly died this young man who was 12 years old a handicapped beggar named Felder Dionysus known around town as dirty animal he was arrested and after he was arrested he told the authorities like hey I know the jackal and yeah he's alive I was just in contact with him a couple weeks ago not only is he alive but he leads a gang of beggars they live out of the slums outside of town he teaches them magic and they're all you know sorcerers together and he's their leader and so from that point they really started hitting hard all the you know begging teenagers and forcing them into these confessions and they never found uh Jacob Koller they never found the jackal. But they came up with no there's nearly 140 people mostly teenagers they got them mostly all to confess to being you know sorcerers and witches and you know to say that they knew Koller just because they were being tortured so really majority of them probably false confessions and it resulted in death anyways and so I mean that right there I think puts you know a lot of negative energy towards the castle it gives a lot of the potential to have hauntings could be haunted by these young men who were tortured and put to death on false accusations they could have something lingering around still. So, especially if you know maybe someone did do magic I don't know they could have been real wizards so maybe they did leave something behind so right there that's a good start for a place to be haunted but then there's more to Moosham Castle than just these witch trials there's also werewolves believed to be at Moosham Castle that where was that that's cool like we're going from witches to werewolves got all the w paranormal stuff going on here and you know I think it's kind of interesting on how the werewolves come about. I've seen uh conflicting dates with the werewolves. So, I don't know if it was two separate werewolf incidents or if it's just you know and over time just dates got kind of construed, I'm not real sure but I always think it might actually be two separate incidents because the accounts are similar but there got their differences to them. Still so initially I found that once these witch hunts kind of stopped there's about a hundred years where things were fairly normal at the castle and then about 1790 the archbishop removed the bailiwick from the area, so the church didn't really have as much presence there. Their church wasn't getting funding so kind of dropped back into a more poverty state there at the castle and with that there's about early 1800s I want to say it was they started finding a lot of cattle and a lot of deer being like brutally mutilated around the castle grounds outside the castle and no one knew why like everyone's like I didn't do it you know I don't know what could have done this this is really strange and so with no one saying hey I know how this happened they all just came to the conclusion this must be werewolves and no one obviously knows confessing to being a werewolf I know I wouldn't confess to it if someone's accusing me of being one and you know destroying the town's cattle supply. So, they came to the conclusion that the werewolves must be the last remaining residents of the castle. The people who still live there they're the werewolves and eventually there were people who got accused and just like the witch trials you know they were put through extreme torture until they came up and confessed and said I'm a werewolf and then they were executed. According to the other accounts that I've read about the werewolves it was about 1715 to 1717 there's this like two year period where same thing the cattle deer in the area kept coming up extremely mutilated and you know they're like hey what's going on I don't know why there's all these cattle and deer you know getting all banged up like this and why are they all you know just dead and so same thing as before they're like hey these uh these must be werewolves in the castle and according to a Joe Nickell he did an investigation of Moosham Castle back in 2007 I believe it was he mentioned this instance of the werewolves in 1715-1717 instance of the werewolves and according to him there actually were two people who they accused and like the witch trials it was two teenage men and they confess to being the werewolves and after being tortured and confessing to it instead of being executed they are allowed to live their days out as galley slaves. So, you know there is a chance that maybe there are still werewolves there if the two known werewolves were allowed to live you know they may pass that werewolf gene on or who knows but yeah that's kind of interesting. So, you got witches and werewolves what else could be going on at Moosham Castle to keep the paranormal going there I mean it seems you got everything so far, I mean hey, but you know what it doesn't end they got the ghost too. There's a ghost at Moosham Castle and this is a kind of interesting tale of one the ghosts who may or may not be there and I find this kind of cool. So just one little back hint here so back to Jacob Koller real fast according to one source that I read his father was an executioner and this story here talks about an executioner who lived at Moosham Castle much later than the witch trials uh this was about the mid-1800s so probably like 150 years give or take from the witch trials but this man Anton who a lot of people called Schorgen-Toni was his nickname and I'm sure I said that completely wrong so please forgive me but you know he was he was straight up an evil man he enjoyed torturing people they said he tortured his own parents you know any prisoners he went to the extreme to torturing them and it was like enjoyment for him and then they say he sold his soul to the devil just from how cruel he was and then as the legend goes one night this mysterious carriage arrived to the castle gates and the gates opened by themselves and let this carriage in the carriage came into the courtyard and a hooded figure came out and that hooded figure came to Toni's door and began knocking and entered the room and there stood this cloaked black figure that he said to Toni good night sir for I am from hell and my prince has ordered me to prepare you for your journey and then as Toni begged at this man not to take him he pleaded not to go with this hooded figure the hooded figure forcibly dragged tony back to the carriage and took him away. And they say that you can still hear Toni there, people say they've seen Toni, they feel a heavy presence in his old room so he may be there haunting the place still as he never left, he just went to hell from there so that that's kind of interesting there's just so much going on at this place.

I want to visit it someday see what kind of energies it's putting off but it's just you know a good round table of all kinds of stuff it's got the witches the werewolves the ghost you know it's got the history of the battles the war taking place there so it is just right to have a haunting and you know I like to visit it someday see what's going on there that's kind of like a quick little summary of what's going on at Moosham Castle I'm glad I found it I look forward to learning more about it and you know if you've ever been there and want to share experience I'd love to hear it leave a review send me an email at potentpuffin@gmail.com leave a comment on YouTube connect with me on twitter I'd love to hear your story for any corrections you might know about this place and the best places I found in my study that had the best write-ups was little house of horrors, dark tourists, and the raven report they all had really good write-ups about this place the raven report really had a lot of good information about the Salzburg which trials I thought so shout out to those places for providing good information for me and that's gonna do it for this week you know hope you enjoyed it I enjoyed sharing this with you and I'll catch you all next time

SELKIES:
The Seal Folk

Hello there and welcome to the Paranormal Puffin a Potent Puffin sideshow and I'm your host Jake Thomas and sitting here beside me is Kita the elkhound. Today I'll be talking about a mythological creature coming from Celtic and Norse mythologies. They are mostly found in the northern isles of Scotland especially around the Orkney archipelago and these are the selkies also known as the seal folk and these are shape-shifting sea creatures that are known as the fae of the sea they change from seals to humans when they shed their seal skin when they come out to land it's often debated how often they're able to come on to land to become humans. Some say that it can only happen once a year some say it's every ninth night they're able to do so there's other variations on how often they're able to come on to land and become human and they say the most likely times for you to be able to encounter a selkie in human form is on mid-summer's night or on all hallows as those are both fae festivals and the selkies like to come ashore to celebrate those festivals as they are a type of fae. They are often depicted as being larger seals with very human-like eyes and sometimes certain pictures being more mermaid like where they're you know part human part seal and then once they're on land they become fully human. But I think they're typically just larger seals is how I generally see them depicted and how I picture them with my mind. Now they're often the subject of stories that are romantic tragedies as probably the most famous tale is the selkie wife. Both stories are kind of variations of this where a female selkie comes ashore and she takes off her seal skin to become human and she's dancing in the moon light and a fisherman who has recently lost his wife and is wanting a mother for his children comes upon her and he takes her skin takes the seal skin from her. So that she is pretty much forced to go with him so that she could try and get it back but selkies can only get their seal skin back if it is given to them willingly. So he holds the skin hostage from her keeping it locked in a chest and she eventually becomes his wife and she takes care of the children and they say that she genuinely loved the children because selkies are gentle creatures and they love to take care of children even those that aren't theirs, and so even though she found fulfillment in taking care of these children she longed to go back to the sea longed to go back to her home and she sat by the window in kind of a depressed state just wanting to go back to the sea and one day the fisherman leaves and he forgets to take the key to the chest and his children are very curious about this chest because they've never seen it opened and they don't know what's inside they see that key and they take it they open the chest to find the seal skin and not knowing that it actually belongs to their stepmother that they don't know that she's truly a selkie they think she's just a woman so she asks the children to have the seal skin and they willingly give it to her so she is able to take it and once she has it she runs to the sea as fast as she can putting on that seal skin and returning to her true seal form and going back to the sea. The fishermen he's angry and he keeps returning to the waterside hoping to find her again but he's not able to as according to the legends that once a selkie has recovered her skin that she's not able to appear to the fishermen again so even though she's right in front of him he is not able to see her and that's basically how the story goes this is kind of a splitting part here is it's often debated what became of her after that. Some say that she just stays in the sea and you know she stays there she minds her own business does her own thing and she's living a fulfilled life in the sea others say that she uh became very vengeful and became a sea witch and extracts her revenge on unsuspecting fishermen and is often attributed with the deaths of fishermen who die at sea which is kind of I find odd because selkies are generally referred to as being gentle and kind creatures unlike other types of water creatures to come from the Celtic regions and so I find that interesting.

Now I kind of talked about it with that story with how female selkies are typically attributed that's generally how stories involving female selkies go is someone takes their seal skin and they're kind of forced to go with them now eventually their seal skin they say always find its way back to the selkie and they're able to return.

There's some you know differing views on what would happen if the selkie were to have their seal skin destroyed as they are immortal as they are a type of fae but they say that if their skin is destroyed some believe that will actually cause them to die others say that just will trap them in their human form and they'll live forever in human form but they'll be in a very kind of distraught and depressed state as they're now trapped in that human form but male selkies on the other hand the roles are kind of reversed.

So, with male selkies they're always described as being extremely attractive and able to be very good at satisfying women and it's often said that they seek out women specifically ones who are unsatisfied so that they can kind of take advantage of them that way. They say that often times unsatisfied women will seek out the selkies to find that satisfaction they say that if a woman were to go to the sea at high tide and shed seven tears that would attract a male selkie to her and he would be able to take care of her in that way. Some stories I've seen they even say that male selkies are very fertile so sometimes women will seek them out for the purpose of becoming pregnant and there are a lot of accounts of women having children from selkies. They say that a selkie male who has children with a human female will disappear for seven years and after seven years he will return to her and take the children back to the sea with him and then once he does that, he will pay the woman. I don't know how he pays her and if that's money or food I don't know I've never found anything about how he pays her, but he will pay her for taking care and raising his children for seven years.

That's kind of you know how the selkies operate and we kind of talk about what they are some people believe that they are fallen angels some early Christian theory states that they were actually souls who were trapped in purgatory and waiting to go through that but the most likely scenario of what the selkies actually are is there are likely Finnish travelers who were traveling in their kayaks because their kayaks were made from seal skin. They also wore seal fur as clothing they would often come ashore and since their clothing would be wet they would take them off to let them dry and I could see you know early Celtic people saying these people these boaters come ashore and you know it looks like they're looks like a giant seal because they're wearing seal fur and then they see the fur come off and there's a human there and so that could be where some of these stories originated. Is just the early Celts interacting with Finnish travelers and you know it makes sense that some of the men of the region would take these Finnish travelers as their wives and they use these stories as the justification for it and you know could also be you know vice versa women who weren't satisfied with the local pool they see these travelers coming and they you know seek out these travelers who they know will be gone soon and again they use the story of the selkie as their justification or reasoning for what has happened and you know where these children that they're about to bear came from without ruining you know their old self their status or whatever.

So I mean that's likely where it is but who knows it could be real they're definitely an interesting creature I enjoyed reading about them and learning about them and yeah that's about all I really have for the selkies if you have any cool stories about the selkies if you've ever encountered one or think you may have encountered one I'd love to hear about it you can reach out to me on twitter at either potentpuffin or at paranormalpuffin I have accounts for both you can reach out to me there or you can email me at paranormalpuffin@gmail.com I'd love to hear your stories and if you enjoyed please leave a review or like or comment you know something let me know that you're enjoying my content and I hope you all enjoyed it I'll catch you all next time and as always yeah have a good day.

www.ingramcontent.com/pod-product-compliance
Lightning Source LLC
Chambersburg PA
CBHW051846250726

48659CB00006B/2053